A Study Guide to…

Private Peaceful
at Key Stage 3

Levels 4-7

By Janet Marsh

V2.4

INTRODUCTION

The material contained in this book is meant to supplement and enhance learning at Key Stage 3. The exercises and tasks will enable teachers of English to offer practice in reading, writing, speaking and listening skills. In addition, there will be opportunities to access background information where appropriate to enhance understanding and appreciation of texts.

Every effort is made to ensure that the information provided in this publication is accurate. It is the policy of Coleridge Press to obtain permission on any copyright material in their publications. The publishers will be glad to make suitable arrangements with any copyright holders whom it has not been possible to contact.

Purchasers may photocopy the sheets in this book provided that they do so only for use within their own institution.

ISBN 978-0-993273-54-4

Text by: Janet Marsh
Design and Layout by: David Jones

Published by Coleridge Press

Copyright © Coleridge Press 2015

A Study Guide to.....
Private Peaceful at Key Stage 3
Levels 4 - 7

Contents

FIVE PAST TEN

Private Thomas [Tommo] Peaceful is a young soldier in the trenches during the First World War. The novel opens with these words:

They've gone now and I'm alone at last. I have the whole night ahead of me and I won't waste a single minute of it. I shan't sleep it away. I won't dream it away either. I mustn't, because every moment will be too precious.

I want to try to remember everything, just as it was, just as it happened. I've had nearly eighteen years of yesterdays and tomorrows and tonight I want to remember as many of them as I can. I want tonight to be long, as long as my life, not filled with fleeting dreams that rush me on towards dawn. Tonight, more than any other night of my life, I want to feel alive.

The book opens with a chapter that asks you to do a lot of **speculation** (guessing). Make some intelligent guesses and answer the following questions:-

1. Why do you think the chapter opens with the time 10.05?
2. Who do you think the "They" might be?
3. Why do you think Tommo wants "tonight to be long"?

Structure of the Novel

The novel is organised with 2 story lines going on. One (with the time given in detail) tells us what is happening in the **PRESENT,** the other tells us of Tommo's **PAST**, his childhood, growing up, joining up, the events that lead up to where he is at present, a soldier in WW1.

What can you remember about your past, your **first day at school?**
Fill in the table to jog your memory, then write 2-3 paragraphs about that first day, giving as much detail as possible.

How old were you?	
Where was the school?	
Who took you?	
What did the school look like?	
What was your teacher like?	
What did you do?	
What were your thoughts?	
Did you want to go back?	

FIRST DAYS AT SCHOOL

Charlie is taking me by the hand, leading me because he knows I don't want to go. I've never worn a collar before and it's choking me. My boots are strange and heavy on my feet. Charlie has told me how terrible this school-place is: about Mr Munnings and his terrible tempers and the long whipping cane he hangs above his desk.

A new boy to add to my **trials** and **tribulations**. Was not one Peaceful enough? What have I done to deserve another one? First a Charlie Peaceful and now a Thomas Peaceful. Is there no end to my **woes**? Understand this, Thomas Peaceful, that here I am your lord and master. You do what I say when I say it. You do not cheat, you do not lie, you do not **blaspheme**. You do not come to school in bare feet. Your hands will be clean. These are my **commandments**.

Yes, sir

We file in past him, hands behind our backs in two lines. "Tiddlers" into my classroom, "Bigguns" into Charlie's. I'm the littlest of the Tiddlers. Most of the Bigguns are bigger than Charlie, fourteen years old some of them. I feel so alone.

Answer these questions on the extract:-

1. Why does Tommo feel that he's choking?
2. Which sentence tells us that Tommo normally runs around in bare feet?
3. What is your impression of Mr Munnings? Look at what he says and the way he speaks. Remember to give evidence for what you say
    e.g. Mr Munnings seems to dislike the Peaceful brothers because he says "What have I done to deserve another one?"
4. Look up and write down the meaning of these words used by Mr Munnings: **trials tribulations woes blaspheme commandments**
5. Tommo went to a village school in Devon. Schools were very different in the early 1900s. **Work with a partner or on your own.** From the information on page 3 write down any differences between schools in the 1900s and schools today.

Thomas, you will be sitting there next to Molly. Your laces are undone. Crying won't do them up, you know.

I can't Miss McAllister.

Can't is not a word we use in my class Thomas Peaceful. We shall have to teach you. You show him, Molly. Molly is the oldest girl and my best pupil. She'll help you.

Molly ties laces very differently from Charlie, more slowly in a great big double knot. She doesn't look up at me while she's doing it and I wish she would. She has hair the same colour as Billyboy, Father's old horse – chestnut brown – and I want to reach out and touch it. She looks up at me and smiles. Suddenly I no longer want to run home. I want to stay here with Molly. I know I have a friend.

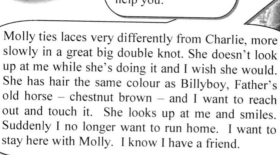

1. Imagine you are teaching someone to tie laces.
   Write down the instructions you would give in point form. You can use drawings to help.
   Start off like this:-
   - Take a lace in each hand.
   - Cross over the laces and tie a single knot.
   - ....

THE FIGHT

1. Read the section in the text that describes the fight with Jimmy Parsons. Explain in your own words:-
   - how Tommo felt about fights in general
   - why Tommo started to attack Jimmy
   - how Big Joe steps in.

2. List the verbs that Tommo uses which describe the actions of Jimmy and Big Joe.

3. Why do you think in a situation like this one, people gather round 'egging them on'?

The cause of this fight is name calling. Jimmy calls Big Joe hurtful names like:-
- loony
- off his head
- off his rocker
- barmy
- nuts

It is clear that Big Joe is different, not only because of his strength.

4. What do you notice about Big Joe's behaviour that marks him out as different from the other Peaceful boys? Think about:-

   - his attitude to animals
   - his singing

Sometimes people are afraid of others who behave differently. They mock them or tease them, sometimes they bully them or make them victims. Even though we know more about the 'differentness' of people like Big Joe today, a hundred years after the time this book is set, the following BBC News article shows that not a lot has changed.
Read it and answer the questions on it.

Mentally ill abused by the young

One in four people experience mental health problems
Six out of ten young people admit verbally abusing the mentally ill, according to a government-backed study.

Out of 500 young people questioned, six out of ten admitted using **derogatory** terms like "psycho, schizo, nutter or loony" to describe the mentally ill.

And even though they considered **racist** language to be **taboo**, only a third felt the terms "psycho and schizo" were unacceptable.

Eighty percent of the young people questioned said they thought having a mental health problem would lead to **discrimination** - despite the fact that one in four people suffer mental health problems during their lives.

1.   Give the meaning of the following words:-

   • derogatory
   • racist
   • taboo
   • discrimination

The Welsh writer Dylan Thomas wrote a series of stories called "Portrait of the Artist as a Young Dog." In *The Fight* he describes how as a boy he was annoying Mr Samuels, a neighbour, when he was suddenly set on by a boy he doesn't know.

I threw a stone at his face. He took off his spectacles, put them in his coat pocket, took off his coat, hung it neatly on the railings, and attacked. Turning round as we wrestled on the top of the bank, I saw Mr Samuels had folded his newspaper on the deck chair and was standing up to watch us. It was a mistake to turn round. The strange boy rabbit punched me twice. Mr Samuels hopped with excitement as I fell against the railings. I was down in the dust, hot and scratched and biting, then up and dancing, and I butted the boy in the belly and we tumbled in a heap. I saw through a closing eye that his nose was bleeding. I hit his nose, He tore at my collar and spun me round by the hair.

"Come on! Come on!" I heard Mr Samuels cry.

We both turned towards him. He was shaking his fists and dodging about in the garden. **He stopped then and coughed, and set his hat straight, and avoided our eyes, and turned his back and walked slowly to the deck chair.**

We both threw gravel at him.

The boy Dylan fought was called Daniel and he and Dylan became lifelong friends.

Quote the details that show us that Daniel is an organised fighter.

1. Who do you think comes off worse in this fight? Give your evidence from the text.
2. How do we know that Mr Samuels is:-
   a. excited by the fight
   b. embarrassed to be seen to be excited?
3. Look again at the sentence in bold. He stopped……chair.
   Why do you think the writer has used 'and' so many times here?
4. "I butted the boy in the belly." What writing technique is used here?
   Why is it effective?

In Tommo's account of the fight he uses details to show what was happening:-

- **fists flailing**
- **curled up like a hedgehog**
- **he puts the boot in**

Now write your own story called 'The Fight'.

You could use the following ideas to give your writing a structure:-
- The setting – **where** and **when** did it happen?
- Who was involved? Were you watching or taking part?
- The reason for the fight if you know - or make it up if it's a good story.
- Was there a crowd? Who else was there?
- What happened?
- How did it end?
- How did you feel?
- Were there any consequences?

Here is someone elses account of a fight.
When I was 16, a mate of mine and I got into a huge argument, which resulted in some shoving. We went outside to fight, surrounded by many in the school, as neither of us had ever been known to fight. We each took couple of swipes at each other, then, after a brief pause, we both looked at each other and began to laugh. Much to the disgust of the spectators! But, we both just realized that what we were doing was entirely silly.

I'm 54 now, and that's the closest I've ever come to a fight. So, it is entirely possible to live a long and happy life without fighting.

Do you agree with this person? Is it possible to go through school and later life without actually having a fight with someone?
Write a paragraph giving your opinion, basing it on your experience if you like.

THE COLONEL AND GRANDMA WOLF

We hadn't liked her before she moved in - as much on account of her moustache as anything else - and we liked her even less now that she had. We had our own name for her. When we were younger Mother had often read us Little Red Riding Hood. There was a picture in it Charlie and I knew well, of the wolf in bed pretending to be Little Red Riding Hood's grandma. She very quickly showed us who was on charge. Now that Mother was not there. Everything had to be done just so: hands washed, hair done, no talking with your mouth full, no leaving anything on your plate. She was so nasty to Big Joe. She talked to him and about him as if he were a baby. She was forever wiping his mouth for him, or telling him not to sing at table.

Using **SCRIPT FORM** write a scene where the family (without Mother, of course) sit down to eat a meal.

Use the characters of Tommo, Charlie, Big Joe, Grandma Wolf, and imagine Molly is visiting too. Make each of your characters speak and act as they would normally do.

Remember:-

- Names in left margin
- No speech marks
- Stage directions in brackets

TEN TO MIDNIGHT
GROWING UP

> I think, without knowing it, I always compared my own growing up to that of Molly and Charlie. Day by day I was becoming painfully aware of how far behind them I was. It wasn't just that I was smaller and slower than they were – the gap was widening and becoming more serious… When I was twelve they left school and I was alone. They both had jobs up in the Big House. Molly was an under - parlour maid and Charlie worked in the stables and the hunt kennels. Molly didn't come round to see us nearly so often as before and, like Charlie, she worked six day a week so I hardly saw her.

Molly was a maid and Charlie worked in the stables and the hunt kennels. Copy out the table below and write down what duties you think Charlie and Molly had to do in their jobs in the Big House.

Charlie's Job	Molly's Job

You need to be a certain type of person to some jobs well. What sort of person would be successful at the following jobs and why?

A police dog handler | would need to be _____

_____

_____

A teacher | would need to be _____

_____

_____

A chef | would need to be _____

_____

A DJ | would need to be _____

_____

_____

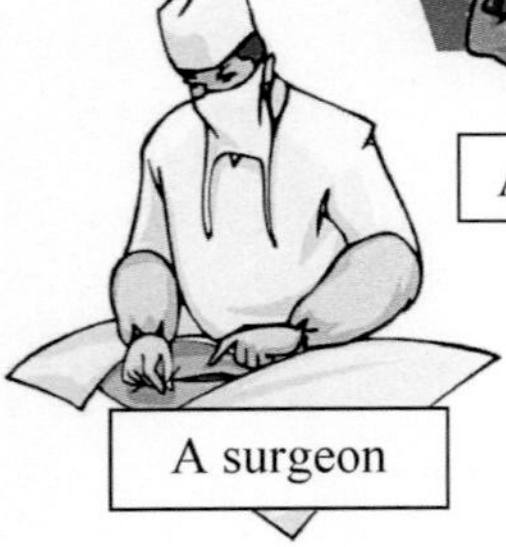

A soldier | would need to be _____

_____

_____

A surgeon | would need to be _____

_____

TWENTY FOUR MINUTES PAST TWELVE

I haven't seen a fox while I've been out here. It's hardly surprising, I suppose. I have heard owls. How any bird can survive in all this I'll never know. I've even seen larks over **no-man's-land**. I always found hope in that.

1. **No-man's-land** is the term used by soldiers to describe the ground between the two opposing trenches. Why is Tommo surprised to have heard owls and seen larks over no-man's-land?

Its width along the Western Front could vary a great deal. The average distance in most sectors was about 250 yards (230 metres). The narrowest gap was at Zonnebeke where British and German soldiers were only about seven yards apart.

No-man's-land contained a considerable amount of barbed wire. In the areas most likely to be attacked, there were ten belts of barbed wire just before the front-line trenches. In some places the wire was more than a 100 feet (30 metres) deep.

If the area had seen a lot of action no-man's-land would be full of broken and abandoned military equipment. After an attack no-man's-land would also contain a large number of bodies. Advances across no-man's-land were always very difficult. Not only did the soldiers have to avoid being shot or blown-up, they also had to cope with barbed-wire and water-filled, shell-holes.

Soldiers were only occasionally involved in a full-scale attack across no-man's-land. However, men were sometimes ordered into no-man's-land to obtain information about the enemy.

2. What were the dangers facing soldiers in no-man's-land?

TWENTY EIGHT MINUTES PAST ONE

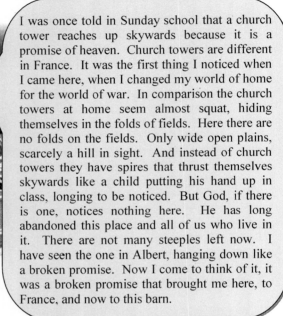

I was once told in Sunday school that a church tower reaches up skywards because it is a promise of heaven. Church towers are different in France. It was the first thing I noticed when I came here, when I changed my world of home for the world of war. In comparison the church towers at home seem almost squat, hiding themselves in the folds of fields. Here there are no folds on the fields. Only wide open plains, scarcely a hill in sight. And instead of church towers they have spires that thrust themselves skywards like a child putting his hand up in class, longing to be noticed. But God, if there is one, notices nothing here. He has long abandoned this place and all of us who live in it. There are not many steeples left now. I have seen the one in Albert, hanging down like a broken promise. Now I come to think of it, it was a broken promise that brought me here, to France, and now to this barn.

1. Tommo has noticed differences in the French landscape since he has been in France. What does he say about:-
   - French church towers?
   - The fields?
   - French church steeples?
2. Pick out 2 examples of SIMILES in this extract.
3. Why do you think Tommo says "But God, if there is one"?
4. In what way might Tommo think coming to France was like a "broken promise"?

THE WEDDING

Molly's come to stay. Charlie, she's going to have your baby. They packed her case, put her out of the door and told her never to come back again. She had nowhere else to go. I said she was family, that she belongs with us now, that she can stay as long as she likes.

That was for me to say. It's our baby, so I should have said it… but I'm glad you said it all the same.

They were married up in the church a short time later. It was a very empty church. There was no one there except the vicar and the four of us, and the vicar's wife sitting at the back. Everyone knew about Molly's baby by now, and because of that the vicar had only agreed to marry them on certain conditions: that no bells were to be rung and no hymns to be sung. He rushed through the marriage service as if he wanted to be somewhere else. There was no wedding feast afterwards, only a cup of tea and some fruit cake when we got home.

1. Why did everyone know about the baby?
2. Why was the marriage different from other weddings celebrated in the church?
3. What is your opinion of the way Molly and Charlie were treated?
4. What do you know about the way weddings are celebrated in Britain nowadays? Write a paragraph which includes:-
   - where people get married
   - how the wedding takes place
   - church/civil ceremonies
   - different traditions to do with weddings.

Have you ever been to a wedding? Even if you haven't you will know enough to be able to imagine what it would be like.

Write a narrative called **The Wedding.** It can either be based on a wedding you have been to or one you could imagine.

PATRIOTIC DUTY

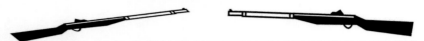

> **While Tommo is at Hatherleigh market one day he sees the following:**
> As I came round the corner I saw them. Behind the band there must have been a couple of dozen soldiers, splendid in their scarlet uniforms. They marched past me, arms swinging in perfect time, buttons and boots shining, the sun glinting on their bayonets. They were singing along with the band: *It's a long way to Tipperary, it's a long way to go.* And I remember thinking it was a good thing Big Joe wasn't there, because he'd have been bound to join in with his *Oranges and Lemons.* Children were stomping alongside them, some on paper hats, some with wooden sticks over their shoulders. And there were women throwing flowers, roses mostly, that were falling at the soldiers' feet. But one of them landed on a soldier's tunic and somehow stuck there. I saw him smile at that.

> Like everyone else, I followed them round the town and up into the square. The band played *God Save the King* and then, with the Union Jack fluttering behind him, the first sergeant major I'd ever set eyes on got up on the steps of the cross, slipped his stick smartly under his arm, and spoke to us, his voice unlike any voice I'd heard before, rasping, commanding.

The purpose of this display is to **RECRUIT** soldiers for the war.
Look carefully at the details and description in this passage to see why young men like Tommo will be affected by it.

Why will young men be influenced by:-

- the uniform?
- what the women are doing?
- what the children watching are doing?
- the sounds they can hear?
- the flag?
- the sergeant major?

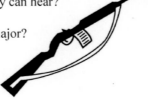

YOUR COURAGE
YOUR CHEERFULNESS
YOUR RESOLUTION
WILL BRING US VICTORY

The sergeant major speaks to the crowd.
"I shan't beat about the bush, ladies and
gentlemen," he began. "I shan't tell you
it's all tickety-boo out there in France -
there's been too much of that nonsense
already in my view. I've been there.
I've seen it myself. So I'll tell you
straight. It's no picnic. It's hard slog,
that's what it is, hard slog. Only one
question to ask yourself about this war.
Who would you rather see marching
through you streets? Us lot or the
Huns? Make up your minds. Because
mark my words, ladies and gentlemen, if
we don't stop them out in France the

Germans will be here, right here in Hatherleigh, right here on your
doorstep."

"They'll come marching through here, burning your houses, killing your
children, and yes, violating our women. They've beaten brave little
Belgium, swallowed her up in one gulp! And they've taken a fair slice of
France too. I'm here to tell you that unless we beat them at their own
game, they'll gobble us up as well." His eyes raked over us. "Well? Do
you want the Hun? Do you?"

This speech is typical of a speech designed to PERSUADE the listener. It
uses techniques to convince the audience and some of these are:-
➤   persuading the listener you are telling the truth
➤   frightening the listener
➤   speaking of the enemy in a negative way
➤   using repetition to emphasise your point
➤   using direct questions to the audience.

1. Copy the following table and fill an example of the following from the sergeant major's speech.

TECHNIQUE	EXAMPLE
Persuading the listener you are telling the truth	
Frightening the listener	
Speaking of the enemy in a negative way	
Using repetition to emphasise your point	
Using direct questions to the audience	

2. Look at these posters from the war. Write down what each one is trying to persuade people to do.

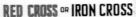

3. Design your own poster using propaganda to persuade people to support one of the following causes:-
   - anti-bullying campaign
   - anti-smoking campaign
   - anti-drug campaign
   - animal rights campaign
   - pro or anti-hunting campaign.

When Charlie is forced by the Major to sign up, Tommo decides to go with him. This is what he says.

"And there was that spark in me newly kindled by these scarlet soldiers marching bravely up the High Street in Hatherleigh, the steady march of their feet, the drums and bugles resounding through the town, the sergeant major's stirring call to arms. Perhaps he had awoken in me feelings I never realized I'd had before, and that I'd had certainly never talked about. It was true that I did love all that was familiar to me. I loved what I knew, and what I knew was my family, and Molly, and the

countryside I'd grown up in. I did not want any enemy soldier ever setting

foot on our soil, on my place. I would do all I could to stop him and to protect the people I loved. And I would be doing it with Charlie. Deep down though, I knew that, more than Charlie, more than my country the band or the sergeant major, it was that toothless old woman taunting me on the square. "Y'ain't a coward, are you? Y'ain't a coward?" The truth was that I wasn't sure I wasn't, and I needed to find out."

1. Write down 5 reasons that Tommo says he had for joining up.
2. Do you think you would have been persuaded as Tommo was? Give your reasons fully in 1-2 sentences.

Imagine you are Molly. Write about how you feel when Charlie and Tommo leave to go to war.
You could start like this:
That was a terrible day, the day we saw the boys off on the train...

FOURTEEN MINUTES PAST TWO

The clues continue to build up as Tommo tells us time is passing.
"It tells me there are three hours and forty six minutes left."
What do you think this means? Left to what?
Let's have a look at the clues so far:-

- he's alone
- he's got no appetite
- there's a mouse there with him
- it's no good wishing for the impossible
- he's lost his belief in God
- time is precious.

In a paragraph write down what you think is happening in the present day story and give reasons for your ideas.

BASIC TRAINING

Read the section in the novel where Tommo describes his training then write a letter home which describes basic training and telling the family how it is all going.

Remember to include:-
- the uniform
- what you have been required to do
- the other men
- how Charlie is
- best wishes to everyone.

Dear Mother and Father

 # FRANCE

Tommo never describes Etaples in much detail. He just says this:

The camp stretched away as far as the eye could see, a tented city, and everywhere I looked there were soldiers **drilling, marching, doubling, crawling, wheeling, saluting, presenting arms.** I had never in my life seen such a bustle of people, never heard such a **racket** of humanity. The air **echoed** with the **din** of **barked** orders and **shrieked** obscenities.

Notice how there is little PHYSICAL detail in the description.

What he concentrates on is:-
- what people are doing - notice the repetition of the verbs
- the noise of the place.

Now using similar techniques, write a paragraph of description about:-

- the playground / yard / public areas of your school at break time
- shopping in town during the sales.

PUNISHMENT - SERGEANT HORRIBLE HANLEY

The bullying Sergeant Hanley takes a dislike to the Peaceful brothers and Charlie is punished for **insubordination.** For that he is given Field Punishment no.1.

Here is a factual and contemporary account of Field Punishment No. 1.

"If a man was sentenced he could be punished in a number of ways. These included Field Punishment Number One, which was known as crucifixion. The offender was kept in irons and attached to a fixed object for up to two hours a day and for a period up to three months. The fixed object was not specified. There were allegations that some men were being attached to the wheels of a gun in positions that were within range of enemy shell-fire."

Source K: from 'Contemporary Accounts of the First World War' by John Simkin (Tressell Publications, 1981).

This is how Tommo expresses it:

All day long Charlie was lashed there in the rain, legs apart, arms spread eagled. As we marched past him, Charlie smiled to me. I tried to smile back, but no smile came, only tears. He seemed to me like Jesus hanging on the cross in the church back home in Iddesleigh.

Which piece of writing makes the stronger impact on you? Why?
Consider:-
- if we know the person involved
- setting / weather
- the reaction of spectators
- choice of words – description
- use of first person narrative.

OBEYING THE RULES

In all walks of life there must be rules and regulations - or must there?

- If you had to come up with three rules only for your school, what would they be? Give reasons for your choice.

- In the future you may well share a flat or house with others. Think of 3 rules for your housemates and explain your choice.

Look up the meaning of ANARCHY.

- **Would you like to go to a school where there are no rules or regulations? Why? Why not?**
- **Does a country need laws? If so, why?**
- **What would happen if there were no laws or rules in society?**

In William Golding's novel "Lord of the Flies", a plane carrying school boys crashes on a deserted island. At first the boys are excited with the adventure of this new life, but in this extract, their leader, Ralph and his friend Piggy gather everyone together for a meeting about how they are going to organize themselves.

"So you see," said Ralph, "We need hunters to get us meat. And another thing."
He lifted the shell on his knees and looked round the sun-slashed faces.
"There aren't any grownups. We shall have to look after ourselves."
The meeting hummed and was silent.
"And another thing. We can't have everybody talking at once. We'll have to have 'Hands up' like at school."

He held the conch before his face and glanced round the mouth.

"Then I'll give him the conch."
"Conch?"

"That's what this shell's called. I'll give the conch to the next person to speak. He can hold it when he's speaking."
"But–"
"Look–"
"And he won't be interrupted: Except by me."
Jack was on his feet.
"We'll have rules!" he cried excitedly. "Lots of rules! Then when anyone breaks 'em–"
"Whee–oh!"
"Wacco!"
"Bong!"
"Doink!".
Ralph felt the conch lifted from his lap. Then Piggy was standing cradling the great cream shell and the shouting died down. Jack, left on his feet, looked uncertainly at Ralph who smiled and patted the log.
Jack sat down. Piggy took off his glasses and blinked at the assembly
while he wiped them on his shirt.
"You're hindering Ralph. You're not letting him get to the most important thing."

1. How do the boys respond to Jack's comment about breaking the rules? What do the boys mean?
2. Is Jack obeying the rules here?
3. How does Ralph react to Jack's breaking of the conch rule?
4. What kind of rules (apart from this one about only one person speaking at a time) do you think the boys will have to agree upon?

A MINUTE PAST THREE

There are more clues here:-

- precious moments
- then you can sleep forever

   What is the significance of the time? What do you think is going on?
   Are your ideas the same as earlier?

As the troops march into Belgium they are encouraged to sing. Singing was good for morale and the songs of World War One have been well documented. Sometimes they had their own tunes but sometimes they were well known tunes set to different words. Often instead of cheery marching tunes they made wry comments on what the average British soldier (Tommy) was experiencing.

'Never Mind'

If the sergeant drinks your rum, never mind
And your face may lose its smile, never mind
He's entitled to a tot but not the bleeding lot
If the sergeant drinks your rum, never mind

When old Jerry shells your trench, never mind
And your face may lose its smile, never mind
Though the sandbags bust and fly you have only once to die,
If old Jerry shells the trench, never mind

If you get stuck on the wire, never mind
And your face may lose its smile, never mind
Though you're stuck there all the day, they count you dead and stop your pay
If you get stuck on the wire, never mind

If the sergeant says you're mad, never mind
P'raps you are a little bit, never mind
Just be calm don't answer back, cause the sergeant stands no slack
So if he says you're mad, well - you are.

'I want to go home'

I want to go home, I want to go home.
I don't want to go in the trenches no more,
Where whizzbangs and shrapnel they whistle
and roar.
Take me over the see, where the *Alleyman*
can't get at me.
Oh my, I don't want to die, I want to go home.

I want to go home, I want to go home.
I don't want to visit la Belle France no more,
For oh the *Jack Johnsons* they make such a
roar.
Take me over the sea, where the snipers they
can't get at me.
Oh my, I don't want to die, I want to go home.

Alleyman = German (from Fr. Allemagne)
Jack Johnson = heavy shell (from a boxer of the same name)

Look at the words of these songs and **using evidence from them,** write a list of what the average British soldier hated and feared about the war.

The troops arrive in Poperinghe which they call Pop and shortly after experience their first real trench. The enemy lines are just two hundred yards away. No-man's-land lies in between.

Here as well as the uncertainty of the German attack they have to contend with rats, lice and rain which produces mud.

Look at these contemporary accounts of what life was like in the trenches.

The daily routine for the men in the trenches was for the most part miserable. It was much like going camping, but with no opportunity to go home to clean up and relax. One of the biggest problems facing the men was the mud. Mud was everywhere including clothes, food and weapons. Muddy water also became a serious enemy to the soldier.

The trench, when we reached it, was half full of mud and water. We set to work to try and drain it. Our efforts were hampered by the fact that the French, who had first occupied it, had buried their dead in the bottom and sides. Every stroke of the pick encountered a body. The smell was awful.

Private Pollard - Memoirs

Our trenches are... ankle deep mud. In some places trenches are waist deep in water. Time is spent digging, filling sandbags, building up parapets, fetching stores, etc. One does not have time to be weary.

Private Livesay – Letter Home 1915

Men were required to stand guard in water that gathered at the bottom of their trenches as deep as their knees or higher. This led to many men developing a condition called trench foot. This condition caused the foot to swell up. You would also lose all feeling in your foot. The most painful aspect of trench foot came when the swelling started to go down.

If you have never had trench feet described to you. I will tell you. Your feet swell to two or three times their normal size and go completely dead. You could stick a bayonet into them and not feel a thing. If you are fortunate enough not to lose your feet and the swelling begins to go down. It is then that the intolerable, indescribable agony begins. I have heard men cry and even scream with the pain and many had to have their feet and legs amputated.

Sergeant Harry Roberts – Post War Interview

As well as mud there were rats.

"I saw some rats running from under the dead men's greatcoats, enormous rats, fat with human flesh. My heart pounded as we edged towards one of the bodies. His helmet had rolled off. The man displayed a grimacing face, stripped of flesh; the skull bare, the eyes devoured and from the yawning mouth leapt a rat."

Report of patrol in no-man's-land

The outstanding feature of the trenches was the extraordinary number of rats. The area was infested with them. It was impossible to keep them out of the dugouts. They grew fat on the food that they pilfered from us, and anything they could pick up in or around the trenches; they were bloated and loathsome to look at. Some were nearly as big as cats. We were filled with an instinctive hatred of them, because however one tried to put the thought of one's mind, one could not help feeling that they fed on the dead.

Stuart Dolden - Memoirs

I can't sleep in my dugout, as it is over-run with rats. Pullman slept here one morning and woke up to find one sitting on his face. I can't face that, so I share Newbery's dugout.

Captain Lionel Crouch – Letter Home 1917

THE STENCH OF THE DEAD BODIES NOW IS AWFUL AS THEY HAVE BEEN EXPOSED TO THE SUN FOR SEVERAL DAYS. MANY HAVE SWOLLEN AND BURST. THE TRENCH IS FULL OF OTHER OCCUPANTS, THINGS WITH LOTS OF LEGS, ALSO SWARMS OF RATS.

Sergeant A. Vine – Diary 1915

Which of these accounts of the rats do you find:-

(A) most shocking?
(B) least shocking?

Give you reasons fully and give examples of particular words or phrases to explain your opinion.

Tommo forms part of a small team whose job it is to cross no-man's-land and take a prisoner from the German trenches. This is how he describes part of the operation after they are returning over no-man's-land with their prisoner.

A machine gun opens up behind us and then rifles fire. There is nowhere to hide so we pretend to be dead. We wait till the light dies and the night is suddenly black again. Wilkie gets us to our feet and we go on running, stumbling until more lights go up, and the machine gunners start up again. We dive into a crater and roll down crashing through the ice into the watery bottom. Then the shelling starts. It seems we have woken up the entire German army. I cower in the stinking water with the German and Charlie, the three of us

clinging together, heads buried in one another as the shells fall all about us. Our own guns are answering now but it is little comfort to us. Charlie and I drag the Hun prisoner out of the water. Either he is talking to himself or he's saying a prayer, it's difficult to tell.

1. What dangers does Tommo face here?
2. How do you think he might feel about "The Hun prisoner"?
3. Another clue here is **"I even sent the padre away."** Why would Tommo be visited by the padre (a minister)?

TWENTY FIVE PAST THREE

Read this factual article about Ypres (the British soldiers called it Wipers) and answer the questions on it.

Ypres The Battle of Ypres (and the numerous battles that surrounded this Flanders town) has become linked forever with World War One. Along with the Battle of the Somme, the battles at Ypres and Passchendaele have gone down in history. The town had been the centre of battles before due to its strategic position, but the sheer devastation of the town and the surrounding countryside seems to perfectly summarise the futility of battles fought in World War One.

The land surrounding Ypres to the north is flat and canals and rivers link it to the coast. The major centre in this part of Flanders was Ypres. Control of the town gave control of the surrounding countryside and all the major roads converged on the town. To the south of the town the land rises to about 500 feet (the Mesen Ridge) which would give a significant height advantage to whichever side controlled this ridge of high land.

British troops entered Ypres in October 1914. They were unaware of the size of the German force advancing on the town. However, numbers did not make up for experience as the Germans used what were effectively students to attack professional British soldiers based north of the town at a place named Langemark. Eyewitnesses claim to have seen the German troops, with just 6 weeks training, with arms linked singing patriotic songs as they advanced towards the British. 1,500 Germans were killed and 600 taken prisoner.

Fierce fighting took place around the town and neither the British nor the Germans could claim to control the area. At a place called Wijtschate (about 10 miles south of Ypres) a German corporal called Adolf Hitler rescued a wounded comrade and won the highest honour a German soldier could win - the Iron Cross. Despite fearsome losses on both sides, neither could dominate the other.

1. Why was Ypres such an important town in WW1?
2. What does "all the major roads converged on the town" mean?
3. Which details show the Germans were far less experienced during the first encounter with British troops at Langemark?
4. Why was it important in world history that "a German corporal called Adolf Hitler won an Iron Cross at Wijtschate"?
5. Rewrite the last sentence in your own words.

British soldiers huddle in the snow just outside of Ypres. The treeless background summarises the bombardment the region suffered from and the conditions the soldiers lived in. The first days of November directly affected the town. Each day Ypres was shelled and civilian casualties were high. This tactic set the scene for what Ypres was to suffer for several more years. By the winter, the Germans had not taken Ypres and heavy rain meant that any movement was impossible as the roads turned to mud. The first battle at Ypres limped to a halt.

6. How do we know from the photograph that the region had suffered massive bombardment?
7. Why was rain so important to the progress of the war?

Tommo's story continues

We're back down in the dugout after stand - to, brewing up when the bombardment starts. It doesn't stop for two whole days. They are the longest two days of my life. I cower there, we all do, alone in our own private misery. We cannot talk for the din. There can be little sleep. When I do sleep I see the hand pointing skywards and it is father's hand, and I wake shaking. Nipper Martin has got the shakes too, and Pete tries to calm him but he can't. I cry like a baby sometimes and not even Charlie can comfort me. We want nothing more than for it to stop, for the earth to be still again, for there to be quiet. I know that when it's over, they'll be coming for us, that I'll have to be ready for them, for the gas maybe, or the flamethrowers, or the grenades, or the bayonets. But I don't mind how they come. Let them come. I just want this to stop. I just want this to be over.

1. Although Tommo is telling the story of events that happened in the past, he uses the **PRESENT** tense (are …has …want) Why do you think this is?
2. Tommo says that they all "cower". What does this mean?
3. Which of these words best describes Tommo's mood before the attack?
   emotional   excited   exhausted   patriotic   resigned

The firing starts all along the line, machine guns and rifle fire, shelling, and I'm firing too. I'm not aiming, just firing, firing. Loading and firing again. And still they do not stop. For a few moments it seems as if bullets do not touch them. They come on towards us, unscathed, an army of invincible grey ghosts. Only when they begin to crumple and cry out and fall do I begin to believe that they are mortal. And they are brave too. They do not falter. No matter how many are cut down, those that are left keep coming. I can see their wild eyes as they reach our wire. It is the wire that stops them. Somehow enough of it has escaped the bombardment. Only a few of them find the gaps and they are shot down before they ever reach our trenches. Those that are left, and there are not many now, have turned and are stumbling back, some throwing away their rifles. I feel a surge of triumph welling inside me, not because we have won, but because I have stood with the others. I have not run.

Which word in this extract means the same as the following:-

1. unharmed   _____
2. to fold up   _____
3. cannot be defeated _____
4. to hesitate   _____
5. to move, falling over _____
6. a sudden move of energy _____
7. a feeling of victory _____
8. being bombed   _____
9. will die   _____
10. rising to the surface _____

Charlie is shot in the foot during the attack and is invalided back home. At first Tommo feels resentful then he gets to know Anna at the bar and makes a friend of her. The bad news is that Sergeant Hanley is to be their new sergeant.

Every one of us hated him like poison, a great deal more than we had ever hated Fritz.

NEARLY FOUR O'CLOCK

A cockerel sounds his early morning call, and tells me what I already know but do not want to believe, this morning will break and soon.

I will have to look death in the face again..........this may be my last sunrise, my last day on earth.

For a while things are quiet in the trenches and even St Hanley can do little to make life any more difficult. The one day there is a gas attack.

"Fix bayonets!" Hanley's yelling while we're still trying frantically to pull on our gas masks. We grab our rifles and fix bayonets. We're on the firestep looking out into no-man's-land, and we see it rolling towards us, this dreaded killer cloud we have heard so much about but have never seen for ourselves until now. Its deadly tendrils are searching ahead, feeling their way forward in long yellow wisps, scenting me, searching for me.
Then finding me out, the gas turns and drifts straight for me. I'm shouting inside my gas mask, "Christ! Christ!" Still the gas comes on, wafting over our wire, through our wire, swallowing everything in its path.

Tommo makes the gas seem much more than a chemical substance here.

Select the words and phrases that suggest the gas is a living being.

In the following poem Wilfred Owen describes a gas attack.

The title of the poem is Latin and means **"it is sweet and noble to die for one's country."** It is a line often found on war memorials which commemorate the dead of both World Wars.

Dulce Et Decorum Est

By Wilfred Owen

Bent double, like old beggars under sacks,
Knock-kneed, coughing like hags, we cursed
through sludge,
Till on the haunting flares we turned out backs,
And towards our distant rest began to trudge.
Men marched asleep. Many had lost their boots,
But limped on, blood-shod. All went lame, all blind;
Drunk with fatigue; deaf even to the hoots
Of gas-shells dropping softly behind.

Gas! GAS! Quick, boys!--An ecstasy of fumbling
Fitting the clumsy helmets just in time,
But someone still was yelling out and stumbling
And flound'ring like a man in fire or lime.--
Dim through the misty panes and thick green light,
As under a green sea, I saw him drowning.

In all my dreams before my helpless sight
He plunges at me, guttering, choking, drowning.

If in some smothering dreams, you too could pace
Behind the wagon that we flung him in,
And watch the white eyes writhing in his face,
His hanging face, like a devil's sick of sin,
If you could hear, at every jolt, the blood
Come gargling from the froth-corrupted lungs
Bitter as the cud
Of vile, incurable sores on innocent tongues,
My friend, you would not tell with such high zest
To children ardent for some desperate glory,
The old Lie: Dulce et decorum est
Pro patria mori.

1. How do we know that the soldiers are tired and defeated in stanza 1? Pick out the words and phrases that tell us.
2. How does the mood change in stanza 2? Give examples of words and phrases that show this change.
3. What happens to the soldier who fumbles with his gas mask in stanza 3? Which words and phrases show the effects of the gas?
4. In stanza 3, why does Owen call DULCE ET DECORUM EST "the old lie"?
5. Choose 3 similes from the poem and try to explain what the poet is trying to convey by using them.

This article gives information about poison gas and its uses in WW1.

Poison gas was probably the most feared of all weapons in World War One. Poison gas was indiscriminate and could be used on the trenches even when no attack was going on. Whereas the machine gun killed more soldiers overall during the war, death was frequently instant or not drawn out and soldiers could find some shelter in bomb/shell craters from gunfire. A poison gas attack meant soldiers having to put on crude gas masks and if these were unsuccessful, an attack could leave a victim in agony for days and weeks before he finally succumbed to his injuries.

It is generally assumed that gas was first used by the Germans in World War One. This is not accurate. The first recorded gas attack was by the French. In August 1914, the French used tear gas grenades containing xylyl bromide on the Germans. This was more an irritant rather than a gas that would kill. It was used by the French to stop the seemingly unstoppable German army advancing throughout Belgium and north-eastern France. In one sense, it was an act of desperation as opposed to a premeditated act that all but went against the 'rules' of war. However, while the French were the first to use a gas against an enemy, the Germans had been giving a great deal of thought to the use of poison gas as a way of inflicting a major defeat on an enemy.

In October 1914, the Germans attacked Neuve Chapelle. Here they fired gas shells at the French that contained a chemical that caused violent sneezing fits. Once again, the gas was not designed to kill rather than to incapacitate an enemy so that they were incapable of defending their positions.

This took place against a background of a war in the west that was still mobile. Once trench warfare had literally dug in, all sides involved in the conflict looked for any way possible to bring movement back into their campaigns. One of the more obvious was to develop a weapon that was so appalling that it would destroy not only an enemy frontline but also the will to maintain troops on that frontline. Poison gas might even provoke a mass mutiny along a frontline thus causing it to collapse. In other words, poison gas was the answer for the war's lack of mobility.

Poison gas (chlorine) was used for the first time at the Second Battle of Ypres in April 1915. At around 17.00 hours on the 22nd April, French sentries in Ypres noticed a yellow-green cloud moving towards them - a gas delivered by artillery shells. They thought that it was a smokescreen to disguise the movement forwards of German troops. As such, all troops in the area were ordered to the firing line of their trench - right in the path of the chlorine. Its impact was immediate and devastating. The French and their Algerian comrades fled in terror. Their understandable reaction created an opportunity for the Germans to advance unhindered into the strategically important Ypres salient. But even the Germans were unprepared and surprised by the impact of chlorine and they failed to follow up the success of the chlorine attack.

1. Which country was responsible for using gas first in WW1?
2. What effect did this gas have on the enemy? What was its chemical name?
3. What effect did the use of gas at Neuve Chapelle have on those who breathed it in?
4. What does "the war was still mobile" mean? How was this different from trench warfare?
5. Explain in your own words why poison gas was the answer to the war's immobility.
6. When and where was chlorine (poison gas) first used?
7. How was this gas "delivered "to the enemy?

Read the part of the chapter where Charlie faces up to Sgt. Hanley and refuses to go over the top.

Now search on YouTube for footage of what it was like to go over the top and watch it...

What are your thoughts about what you see here?

Refusal to obey an order was a court martial offence. Charlie knows the consequences of his action and tells his brother what he wants him to do.

Just listen, Tommo, will you? I want you to promise me you'll look after things for me. You understand what I'm saying? You promise?

Tommo will look after Molly and little Tommo - if he survives. In addition, Charlie gives his brother his most treasured possession, his watch.

Can you see the importance of the chapter headings now?

They did not let me see him for another six weeks, and by then the court martial was all over, the death sentence passed and then confirmed. That was all I knew, all anyone knew, I knew nothing whatever of how it had all happened until yesterday, when at last I was allowed to see him.

They had their one witness, Sergeant Hanley, and he was all they needed. It wasn't a trial, Tommo. They'd made up their minds. I was guilty even before they sat down. I had three of them, a brigadier and two captains looking down their noses at me as if I was some sort of dirt. I told them everything, Tommo, just like it happened. I had nothing to be ashamed of, did I? I wasn't going to hide anything. So I told them that, yes, I did disobey the sergeant's order because the order was stupid, suicidal - we all knew it was - and that anyway I had to stay behind to look after you.

Do you think Charlie was guilty? Act out the scene where Charlie is brought before the court martial. You will need people to play:-

Charlie   Sergeant Hanley   The Brigadier   Captain1   Captain 2

REMEMBER to speak as these people might speak.

Shot for cowardice, desertion and insubordination - or murdered for shell shock?

Combat stress, war neurosis, shell shock.

Never in the field of human conflict has so little been gained by the death of so many.

During the Great War of 1914-1918 around 9 million men lost their lives in one of the greatest acts of barbarity and futility the world has ever seen. This compares to an estimated 14 million deaths during all wars in the previous century. The heroism and sacrifice of troops in the trenches is probably <u>without parallel</u>. However, during the war, 306 British and Commonwealth soldiers were shot on the orders of <u>military top brass</u> and senior officers. In contrast, the Germans only executed 25 of their own. The Americans executed none of their soldiers.

1. **What does "without parallel" mean?**
2. **What does "military top brass" mean?**
3. **What point is the article trying to make when it says that the Germans only executed 25 of their soldiers and the Americans none?**

The pretexts for execution for British soldiers had a common theme: many were suffering shell shock (also called "war neurosis" or "combat stress" and now recognised as Post Traumatic Stress Disorder or PTSD), and most were deliberately picked out and convicted "as a lesson to others". Charges included desertion, cowardice, or insubordination (any minor action that could be pressed into service as an excuse for execution). Most of those shot were young, defenceless and vulnerable teenagers who had volunteered for duty. They were selected, charged, and subjected to a mock trial often without defence, one day convicted, then shot at dawn the following day. <u>Eye-witness accounts suggest many faced their death with a gallantry absent in their accusers.</u>

4. What does the underlined sentence mean?

General Haig, when questioned, declared that all men accused of cowardice and desertion were examined by a Medical Officer (MO) and that no soldier was sentenced to death if there was any suspicion of him suffering shell shock. In fact, most soldiers accused of cowardice and desertion were *not* examined by an MO, and in the few cases where a medical diagnosis of shell shock had been made, the medical evidence was rubbished or ignored and the man was convicted and shot anyway. General Haig not only signed all the death warrants but when questioned later on this issue lied repeatedly. General Haig's behaviour in choosing to murder his own men places him in the category of war criminal.

5. **This section of the article is very critical of General Haig. It firstly accuses him of lying. What did he lie about, according to the article?**

6. **It also accuses him of being a war criminal. What evidence does it give to support this?**

So obsessed were British Generals with making accusations of cowardice and malingering that it is more likely to be projection; weak, inadequate, cowardly, but aggressive individuals project their weaknesses onto others in order to distract and divert attention away from their own weakness and inadequacy. <u>This mentality still thrives in employers who blame employees suffering stress for not being able to cope with their job and for being weak and inadequate. Anyone indulging in a blame - the - victim strategy is revealing their own inadequacy.</u>

7. **In this section of the article there is change of direction. Instead of being simply about desertion in WW1 it becomes a piece of writing about a wider issue. What is that issue? In your own words sum up what you think the underlined section means.**

Documentation on these atrocities was kept secret for 75 years and only recently have the circumstances become clear. In the intervening period, the families of these men have suffered shame, humiliation and embarrassment, compounded by the government's refusal to allow the families to mourn these men alongside their comrades. For these families, an awful guilty secret has blighted their lives and financial hardship has been heaped upon them through the actions of neighbours, landlords, employers and gossips exhibiting the prejudice of a misinformed public.

8. **This section deals with the unfair treatment that the families of those executed have suffered. Explain what this unfair treatment has meant to the families.**

The shooting of 306 British and Commonwealth World War 1 soldiers for spurious reasons remains one of the grossest unresolved injustices of the last 100 years and is exceeded only by the compounded injustice of successive governments' refusal to grant these men posthumous pardons such that their names can be cleared and their families and descendants can mourn their loss.

There is nothing to be achieved by continuing this policy of refusal. The British Government now needs to do the decent thing and admit that the Policy of refusal to pardon was a mistake. Only when posthumous pardons are granted can forgiveness and healing begin.

Progress is being made. In the year 2000, relatives of the 306 murdered soldiers were allowed, for the first time, to march alongside World War 1 veterans on Remembrance Day and lay wreaths at the Cenotaph in London.

9. **What is a posthumous pardon?**
10. **What progress was made in 2000?**

The horrific loss of life in WW1 was due largely to the incompetence and abuse by officers (situated a safe distance from the fighting), military top-brass (situated at an even safer distance from the fighting) and government officials and ministers (situated in a different country).

The principal strategy in trench warfare was to send troops over the top to walk across no-man's-land with the objective of reaching the enemy's trenches and shooting them. The distance between front-line trenches varied from a few yards to several hundred yards or more. However, the ground between the trenches was usually flat, exposed, without cover, deep in mud, littered with bodies and body parts, remains of ordnance, shell holes and barbed wire. The enemy were equipped with machine guns, who with unimpeded vision could mow down approaching troops with small risk to themselves.

One could understand General Haig relying on this tactic for a couple of weeks, even a couple of months. He was following strategies recommended in his military textbooks whereby battles until then had been fought in this manner.

But why did it not dawn upon him that sending a battalion of troops over the top and walking through exposed territory that virtually every soldier would be shot by machine gun fire before reaching the enemy's trenches? If any soldier did make it to the opposing trenches he would be able to shoot perhaps one or two enemy before himself being shot. In other words, the likely kill ratio is probably 50-1 or more. For every enemy soldier killed, 50, perhaps 100 of your own soldiers would be killed.

This last section is highly critical of General Haig and his generals and the tactics they used to conduct the war.
11. **How does it criticise sending troops over the top into no - man's - land?**
12. **Why does the article say General Haig used these tactics?**
13. **What do these words and phrases mean:-**
   • **principal strategy**
   • **unimpeded vision**
   • **exposed territory**
   • **the likely kill ratio**

Tommo visits his brother before he faces the firing squad. Tommo tells him how he still blames himself for their father's death, but Charlie tells him he is not guilty of it.
Finally Charlie hands Tommo a letter for Molly and one for his mother.
Write those letters.

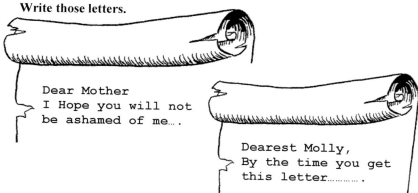

Dear Mother
I Hope you will not
be ashamed of me... .

Dearest Molly,
By the time you get
this letter............ .

As his brother faces the firing squad, Tommo, now billetted near an empty farmhouse less than a mile from Walker Camp, wants to be alone as he imagines how it will be when at six o'clock his brother faces death - not just death but death with dishonour.

Executed WW1 soldiers to be given pardons

All 306 British First World War soldiers executed for desertion or cowardice are to be pardoned, Des Browne, the defence secretary, will announce today.

For 90 years, families, friends and campaigners for the young soldiers have argued that their deaths were a stain on the reputation of Britain and the army.

In many cases, soldiers were clearly suffering from shellshock but officers showed no compassion for fear that their comrades would have disobeyed orders and refused to go "over the top".

Defence sources said last night that Mr Browne regards all of them as victims of the First World War. Whatever the specific legal and historical considerations, it was fundamentally a moral issue which had stigmatised the families involved for more than a generation, he concluded.

The only distinction he is likely to make is between the soldiers shot for cowardice and desertion and others who were executed for murder.

The pardons will need a decision by parliament and Mr Browne is likely to append it to the armed forces bill on what ministers hope will be a free vote.

Andrew Mackinlay, Labour MP for Thurrock, who has campaigned for the pardon, welcomed the move last night and said that public opinion had "moved remarkably in support of a pardon".

He said: "All the courts martial were flawed. People did not have a chance to produce evidence or call witnesses. Full marks to Des Browne, but the point is that it has taken the British establishment 90 years."

1. How long have friends and families of the executed soldiers been campaigning?
2. What does a *stain on the reputation of Britain and the army* mean?
3. What does *had stigmatized the families involved* mean?
4. What do you think a *free vote* means?
5. Why does the article quote the **actual words** of Andrew Mackinlay and not just say *Andrew Mackinlay said that he*..........

The firing squad stands at ease, waiting. Six men, their rifles loaded and ready, each one wanting only to get it over with. They will be shooting one of their own and it feels to them like murder. They try not to look at Charlie's face.

Charlie is tied to a post. The padre says a prayer, makes the sign of the cross on his forehead and moves away. It is cold now but Charlie does not shiver. The officer, his revolver drawn, is looking at his watch. They try to put the hood over Charlie's head, but he will not have it. He looks up to the sky and sends his last living thoughts home. "Present! Ready! Aim!"

Write an account of Charlie's death from the point of view of:-

- the padre
- one of the firing squad
- the officer

We leave Tommo marching with his regiment up to the Somme. Will he survive to get back to 'Blighty' and his family? The novel offers us no answer.

Extended Tasks on the Book

Using the Internet, collect information and present it in a 3 - 4 minute talk to the group on one of the following topics:-

- why the war started
- the part played by women in WW1
- weapons used in WW1
- propaganda
- Wilfred Owen
- shell shock - causes and treatment
- 3 poems by poets other than Owen - discuss them with the class.

REMEMBER:-
➤ You are going to talk to your peer group so use language they will understand.
➤ Don't just read off lots of information straight from web pages. Edit and where necessary reword the information.
➤ Use visual aids if it is appropriate, like maps, artefacts, Power Point
➤ Become so familiar with your material than you can look up confidently from time to time and make eye contact with your audience.

Useful sites;
www.bbc.co.uk
www.firstworldwar.com
www.historylearningsite.co.uk
www.europeanhistory.about.com
www.historyonthenet.com

Private Peaceful **offers us no nice easy, happy ever after ending. We will never know if Tommo will get home and pick up the threads of his old life. Even if he does, he will never be the same again.**
At the end of the book Tommo is on his way to the Somme which does not make us feel too hopeful.

Find out about the Battle of the Somme and write a short entry (200 words) to be included in a history text book intended for 11 year olds. Pupils who have read *Private Peaceful* **have written and sent their reviews to the following website: www.amazon.co.uk**

SATIRE

Some of those who wrote poetry in WW1 did so to SATIRISE what was happening in the hopes of showing up the fatal blunders that cost so many lives. **Satire** has long been a way of producing **black humour for the purpose of making a serious point.**

If you have ever seen **"Blackadder Goes Forth"** you will remember that blend of humour and criticism – and you will surely remember the final episode where Blackadder etc. go over the top with the words **"The Great War - 1914 to 1917."**

Siegfried Sassoon wrote the following poem as satire.

The General

"Good-morning; good-morning!" the General said
When we met him last week on our way to the line.
Now the soldiers he smiled at are most of 'em dead,
And we're cursing his staff for incompetent swine.
"He's a cheery old card," grunted Harry to Jack
As they slogged up to Arras with rifle and pack.

But he did for them both by his plan of attack.

1. What is the General's attitude to the soldiers?
2. What do they think of him?
3. What does the last line mean?
4. The poet uses a strong rhyme in the poem and a strong rhythm. What is the effect of this when you read the poem?

Military Casualties of World War 1

Country	Dead	Wounded	Missing	Total
Australia	58,150	152,170	-	210,320
Austria-Hungary	922,000	3,600,000	855,283	5,377,283
Belgium	44,000	450,000	-	494,000
Britain	658,700	2,032,150	359,150	3,050,000
Bulgaria	87,500	152,390	27,029	266,919
Canada	56,500	149,700	-	206,200
France	1,359,000	4,200,000	361,650	5,920,650
Germany	1,600,000	4,065,000	103,000	5,768,000
Greece	5,000	21,000	1,000	27,000
India	43,200	65,175	5,875	114,250
Italy	689,000	959,100	-	1,424,660
Japan	300	907	3	1,210
Montenegro	3,000	10,000	7,000	20,000
New Zealand	16,130	40,750	-	56,880
Portugal	7,222	13,751	12,318	33,291
Romania	335,706	120,000	80,000	535,706
Russia	1,700,000	5,000,000	-	6,700,000
Serbia	45,000	133,148	152,958	331,106
Turkey	250,000	400,000	-	650,000
USA	58,480	189,955	14,290	262,725
Totals	**7,996,888**	**21,755,196**	**1,979,556**	**31,508,200**

Using the table of statistics, answer the following:-
1.   Which country suffered the highest losses of dead and wounded?
2.   Which of these countries listed suffered the lowest?
3.   Australia and New Zealand are a long way away from the Theatre of War (France and Belgium). Why did they suffer heavy losses?
4.   Can you name any of the countries listed here that no longer exist?

1. Search on the internet for a trailer of the film *Private Peaceful* and watch it, then answer the following questions:-

If you were producing a trailer for a film like *Private Peaceful*, what must you bear in mind about:-

- which scenes to show
- the variety of scenes to show
- the dialogue you will show
- the scenes in which well-known stars appear
- music
- what you reveal of the plot.

Here are 2 reviews of the film. Read through them carefully then answer the questions that follow.

A

Film Review: 'Private Peaceful'

★★★☆☆

Pat O'Connor's *Private Peaceful (2012)* is a finely-told story of two young brothers, battling the ups and downs of childhood, the confusion and difficulties in adolescence and two of the more troubling things that could happen during the life of a young man: fighting a war for your country and falling in love. With some seriously fine performances and a simple but effective visual style that helps establish the film as a believable period piece, O'Connor's film is a solid adaptation of Michael Morpurgo's novel.

Set in the Devonshire countryside during the years leading up to the First World War, *Private Peaceful* is a classic rites of passage story about Charlie and Tommo Peaceful and the exuberance and pain of their teenage love for the same girl, along with the pressures of their feudal family life, the horrors and folly of the ensuing war and the ultimate price of courage and cowardice.

As older brother Charlie, Jack O'Connell's performance is wonderfully British and acutely in tune with the way a boy of this time would speak. He plays the strong, self-assured, nurturing and loving brother with genuine effect and subtlety, as his character serves as both role model and antagonist to younger sibling, Tommo, played by George MacKay, who also gives a sterling performance, providing an effective complement and contrast to O'Connell's Charlie. Providing the love dilemma for the two brothers, and much more than that, is an elegant and fine performance from rising talent, Alexandra Roach, who plays the endearing tom-boy, Molly Monks.

It's obvious what O'Connor was trying to achieve and through the film's simplicity, fine performances and well-written screenplay, *Private Peaceful* is a delicate and warm portrayal of love for family, for friends, and for one's country.

1. What do the following words and phrases mean?
   - believable period piece
   - rites of passage
   - the ensuing war
   - younger sibling.

B A story of family, love and growing up, *Private Peaceful* is a touching yet harrowing watch.

★★★☆☆

Adapted from the book by Michael Morpurgo, the film follows Tommo Peaceful on one night as he looks back on his life.

The beginning of the film is ominous, starting as it does during the First World War with a sentence being handed down for disobeying orders given in the field.

That sense of dread stays with the audience through the rest of the film, even through happier scenes, and at times the constant misery gets a bit too much.

Young Tommo and Charlie Peaceful, played by child actors Samuel Bottomley and Hero Fiennes-Tiffin, defend each other through thick and thin, have a good home life with their loving parents and older brother, and meet the girl of their dreams, Molly, when both are at school.

Their happy life is shattered when their father dies in a tragic accident, and both boys go to work for the Colonel, the richest man in the village they live in.

Richard Griffiths is amusing as the overblown Colonel, whose lazy behaviour and rants on responsibility provide a comic edge to tragic proceedings, but he disappears two thirds of the way through the film, as the plot dispenses with the need for his character, and it's a loss that's certainly felt.

As they grow older Tommo, played as a teenager by George Mackay, finds himself falling more and more in love with Molly, who in turn is in a relationship with his brother, all against the backdrop of the fast-approaching First World War.

Heading off to the trenches, Tommo tries to find a place for himself as he grows into adulthood on the battlefield, surrounded by death and destruction wrought not just by the enemy, but by his own side in the shape of Sergeant Hanley.

John Lynch is formidable as Sergeant Hanley, who has a personal vendetta against the Peaceful boys and whose viciousness is the catalyst to the final heart-breaking scenes of the film.

Watching him emerge from the smoke on the battlefield, crawling his way back to the trenches is spooky, and enough to put fear in the hearts of the bravest souls as the climax of the film approaches.

Private Peaceful is moving, from the scenes on the battlefield to the smaller moments of heartbreak at home, but does leave viewers feeling despondent. Have tissues on hand when watching.

2.   What do the following words and phrases mean?

- harrowing
- the plot dispenses with the need for his character
- formidable
- vendetta
- despondent.

3. Now think about both reviews and in columns A and B, note the
    following points:-

    - when the film is set
    - which actor plays Charlie
    - the part played by Richard Griffiths
    - the name of the director
    - the most complimentary thing that each review says of the film
      overall
    - the least complimentary thing each says.

A	B